Simply Anxious:
The Little Book of Comfort

A wealth of lived experience, comforting insights and inspiring posts that led to the author's healing and recovery from debilitating anxiety.

LISA TOWERS

Disclaimer:

The content shared in this book is drawn from my personal journey of grappling with and overcoming anxiety. It serves as a reflection of my individual experiences and the lessons learned during the process of recovery. It is important to note that this information is for personal insights and awareness only. If you find yourself grappling with mental health challenges, it is crucial to seek professional assistance. Always consult with a qualified mental health professional who can provide tailored guidance and support based on your unique situation. Your well-being is of utmost importance, and this book is not a substitute for professional advice and care.

Simply Anxious: The Little Book of Comfort. A self-help guide and source of comfort for those suffering from Anxiety.

Copyright © 2023 by Lisa Towers

All rights reserved.

No part of this book may be reproduced or transmitted in any form or by any means without written permission from the author.

To all who suffer. I see you.

You are not alone, and it will get better.

Table of Contents

Introduction 1

The Power of Believing You Can 2

You Are Not An Anxious Person 3

The Power of Possibility 5

A collection of post to give comfort and hope 7

Anxiety at Christmas 62

A letter to myself 78

How to Build Your Inner Strength 87

Finding Hope 90

Embracing Slow Healing 92

I Will Leave You With This - A Glimmer of Hope 94

Journalling prompts to help explore and reflect: 96

Introduction

In a world brimming with relentless challenges and ceaseless chaos, there exists a silent struggle that many face in solitude: anxiety. It creeps into our minds unannounced, shrouding us in doubt, fear, and apprehension. But it's time to unveil a brighter path, one paved with resilience, hope, and unwavering support.

Welcome to "Simply Anxious: Little Book of Comfort." This book is a tapestry woven from the threads of lived experience, heartfelt wisdom, and the empowering stories shared on my Simply Anxious Instagram Page. Within these pages, you'll find some of my best, most comforting, and most empowering posts, whichever page you flick on.

I, too, have danced with anxiety's relentless grip, and it's in those moments of vulnerability and strength that this book was born. Through self-help tools, practical tips, and the wisdom garnered from both personal battles and my role as an anxiety advocate, I invite you to embrace your anxiety, empower your spirit, and evolve into the resilient, thriving individual you were meant to be.

Written in a voice that seeks to comfort and inspire, I'll guide you through the often tumultuous journey towards recovery. Together, we'll challenge the stigma surrounding anxiety, shatter its myths, and give validation to the depth of this struggle. Whether you're just beginning your journey or have been navigating it for years, this book is a trusted companion, offering solace and strength when you need it most. Allow this book to be your best friend in those challenging times.

Lisa x

The Power of Believing You Can

I want to emphasise one of the most powerful tools I had in my self-help toolkit: the power of belief. It may sound simple, but the impact of your thoughts and beliefs on your ability to recover from anxiety cannot be overstated. Henry Ford once famously said, "Whether you think you can or you think you can't, you're right." This sentiment holds true, especially when it comes to managing and ultimately conquering anxiety.

To understand the significance of belief in recovering from anxiety, we must first acknowledge the intricate relationship between our thoughts, beliefs, and emotional well-being. Anxiety often thrives in an environment of doubt and uncertainty. It feeds on negative self-talk, convincing us we are powerless and incapable of change. This negative self-talk becomes a self-fulfilling prophecy, reinforcing our anxiety and preventing us from taking meaningful steps towards recovery.

Our beliefs about anxiety, ourselves, and our capacity to heal are pivotal in determining our outcomes. If we believe that anxiety is an insurmountable obstacle and that we are helpless victims of our own minds, we inadvertently contribute to our own suffering. On the contrary, if we shift our beliefs to acknowledge that anxiety is a challenge we can conquer, we empower ourselves to take action and regain control over our lives. Don't believe me? Give it a try and see.

You Are Not an Anxious Person

It's important not to define ourselves as "Anxious People" because that label isn't accurate or beneficial. I spent a long time believing I was destined to be an anxious person, living with anxiety and panic disorder indefinitely. Unfortunately, this belief hindered my recovery for quite a while. People's comments, like being labelled as "oversensitive" or a "drama queen," only reinforced this perception and didn't contribute positively.

The more I delved into understanding anxiety and its causes, the more I questioned the label I had placed on myself. Maybe I wasn't inherently anxious; perhaps I didn't have to be stuck like this forever. The prognosis from my doctor, accompanying my diagnosis, had tried to convince me otherwise, suggesting I was just an anxious person destined to be that way forever.

Yes, I was dealing with anxiety and panic disorder, but that didn't define who I was. It was a response to various unresolved issues, trauma, stress at home and work, and an unhealthy lifestyle. Meeting a holistic anxiety therapist confirmed this, opening up a world of possibilities for me. My suffering wasn't about being an anxious person; it was a combination of issues I needed to address, heal from, and change.

The stigma around mental health and the pressure to pretend everything was okay impacted my recovery more than anything. The label made me feel obligated not to show anxiety around others, adding more stress. I don't believe in "faking it until you make it," especially with anxiety. We should feel free to be open and honest about our struggles, receiving the support and compassion we deserve, which is crucial for recovery.

So, I want to tell you that you are not an anxious person. There are multiple factors that can contribute to your struggles, and none of them are insurmountable. Please let go of any label suggesting your battle with anxiety defines you and give yourself the time and space to heal. Ignore the stigma and start making radical changes to overcome what's kept you stuck in your recovery.

Your life is important. You matter. Make your recovery a priority. It's possible to overcome anxiety; you just need to believe it. Even when you feel broken or damaged, you are not. Acknowledging this is crucial for you to recover. You're experiencing a sensitised nervous system, mental fatigue, and emotional exhaustion—all of which can be healed. They are not permanent states; though they cause distress, they cannot harm you.

I spent years thinking I was broken because nobody told me otherwise. After trying countless "anxiety cures" that failed, I felt increasingly unfixable. What I didn't know then was that I didn't need fixing. I could heal myself with the right guidance, support, and time and space. These realisations changed the course of my recovery journey.

Healing anxiety takes time. Understanding and accepting what's happening, learning the facts, and shifting your perception requires time. Anxiety can't hurt you but fearing it can negatively impact your life. You need space to heal, allowing your mind and nervous system to rest and settle.

Support and encouragement are vital. Having someone in your corner showing compassion, love, and encouragement is empowering. This journey might be tough at times, so this support is invaluable. So, please replace the words "broken" and "unfixable" with "mentally and emotionally exhausted" and "I'm in the process of healing" because these better align with the truth.

The Power of Possibility

Anxiety may feel like a heavy burden, an unwelcome companion that casts shadows over your days. Yet, within you resides an innate strength, a wellspring of resilience that can guide you towards the light at the end of the tunnel, no matter how dark it may seem.

Imagine a seed planted in the soil. In the beginning, it's just a tiny, vulnerable entity. Yet, with the right conditions—nourishment, sunlight, and time it grows into a strong tree, firmly rooted in the earth. Similarly, your mindset is the fertile ground where your recovery can take root. Embrace the belief that, despite the storms that may rage around you, you have the power to heal and blossom into a more emotionally aware and resilient version of yourself.

Anxiety thrives on the uncertainty of the future, on the fear of what might happen. These are stories of the mind, not truths. Challenge those fears with the certainty that you possess the tools to weather any storm. It's not about denying the existence of difficult emotions but about recognising your ability to navigate through them. It's not about never experiencing anxiety again but instead knowing how to respond in a non-fuelling way if it does show up.

Imagine your mind as a garden. You can cultivate positivity, plant seeds of hope, and nurture them into thriving, empowering thoughts. When the weeds of doubt and negativity take root, remember that you are the gardener of your mind. You can pluck them out and replace them with seeds of resilience, self-compassion, and empowerment. Keep working at this, and it will become second nature.

Always remember that recovery is not a linear path. It's a journey filled with moments of triumph and moments of self-doubt. Understand that setbacks are not roadblocks but detours, opportunities to recalibrate, reassess, and recommit to your healing journey. Each step forward, no matter how small, is a testament to your strength and courage.

And don't forget to surround yourself with a support system, a network of people who understand the journey. Share your struggles, celebrate your victories, and let the collective energy of gentle encouragement and understanding propel you forward. You are not alone; hands are always reaching out, hearts are willing to listen, and minds are ready to understand.

Believing in your ability to recover is a beacon that will cut through the darkness. When nurtured, it's a flame that can dispel the shadows of anxiety and emotional unrest. Embrace the mindset that recovery is not only possible but inevitable. Your journey may be challenging, but within you lies the power to transform adversity into strength, fear into courage, and unrest into peace.

So, my friend, water those seeds of hope, embrace the power to recover with open arms, and let the healing journey begin.

A collection
of posts to
give comfort
and hope

Anxiety Recovery

Surviving in Survival Mode is an exhausting journey. Each day begins with the weight of dread, inundated with negative thoughts and an overwhelming sense of fear as if life itself has become an arduous battle.

We find ourselves trapped in this relentless cycle due to the unresolved emotional energy that lingers within us, perpetuated by our anxiety-driven behaviours and the ceaseless stressors of everyday life. Over time, this takes a toll on our delicate nervous system.

These suppressed emotions continue to wire our nervous system, keeping our stress hormones in a perpetual state of elevation. Regrettably, many of us remain ensnared in this hyper-sensitized condition for far longer than we should, leading to the onset of anxiety, panic attacks, depersonalization, and more.

The reasons so many of us find ourselves in this predicament are twofold:

We lack the knowledge and tools to process our emotions effectively, and when we do attempt, we seldom allocate the time required for true healing.

Our society thrives on stress, normalizing it to such an extent that living in a perpetual state of high alert has become the new normal.

If you resonate with the feeling of merely surviving, remember that it does not imply something fundamentally wrong with you that requires fixing. Instead, it signals that it's time to prioritise your mental and emotional well-being, granting yourself the necessary time and space to mend your nervous system and restore its equilibrium.

Embracing this commitment may be the most challenging step, for every thought in our minds will insist we keep pressing forward (that's the voice of anxiety!) or that there's something gravely wrong with us. Yet, this is precisely why we must take control, slow down, and extend kindness to ourselves, allowing us the opportunity for genuine recovery.

Daily Habit:

Focus on self-soothing, grounding techniques and slowing your pace.

IF YOU'RE FEELING ANXIOUS –
keep it simple

Keeping things simple when you're anxious is where you want to be. It minimises the risk of getting overwhelmed with those secondary fears.

Remember, all you need to do is allow yourself to return to calm, and that will happen more swiftly when you release the urge to control, fix, analyse, or resist.

I promise you that the simpler you make it, the less time you waste on the things that may seem helpful but ultimately aren't.

Please keep it simple, trust that you are safe and remember, this feeling will eventually pass.

In my healing journey, I realised the things that truly matter and those that don't. Anxiety can cloud our judgment and amplify our worries, making focusing on what deserves our attention and energy challenging.

I learned that:

- **Connection matters.** Surrounding yourself with people who genuinely care, love, and support you can make a world of difference. Lean on your tribe and let their energy uplift you.

- **Self-care matters.** It's essential. Make time for things that bring joy and nourish your mind and body.

- **Perspective matters.** Remind yourself that anxious

thoughts are not a reflection of reality. Reframe negative thinking patterns and work on your mindset. You are capable of overcoming any challenge that comes your way.

- **Letting go matters.** Release the need to control everything. Embrace the uncertainty and surrender to life's flow. Sometimes, the most beautiful things come when we let go and allow things to unfold naturally.

- **Love matters.** Learn to Love yourself unconditionally. Kindness, compassion, and empathy have healing power.

Remember, there will be so many things that don't deserve our attention. Focus your energy on what truly matters to you, and watch your healing journey bloom.

Anxiety doesn't mean you're...

Weak, a burden, stupid, lazy, damaged, unloveable, unworthy abnormal, incapable. doomed

It means you are a human being who needs time and space to rest, heal, and recover away from life's nonsense

I'm so fed up with the ongoing stigma around anxiety! I experienced it firsthand again this week!

I NEED you to know that having anxiety doesn't make you weak, damaged, or less valuable. It's incredibly common nowadays. You're not alone; people from all walks of life experience this. It makes you wonder, is it a mental illness or a reflection of our society?

I believe it's the latter. The pressure of societal expectations, lack of understanding about emotional well-being, and insufficient time and space for healing and self-care all contribute.

You don't need to define yourself with negative labels. Instead, empower yourself and practice self-compassion.

You're unique, and amazing and deserve all the love and support while dealing with anxiety. Taking time for yourself isn't selfish; it's necessary. So, prioritise your well-being without guilt, take all the time you need to heal and don't hesitate to seek help if you need it.

Remember ♥

ANXIETY IS A MESSAGE, AN EMOTIONAL RESPONSE

IT IS TRYING TO GUIDE, NOT HURT YOU

WHEN ACKNOWLEDGED & PROCESSED, IT WILL HEAL

YOU ARE SAFE TO LISTEN & LEARN FROM IT

IT ALWAYS PASSES, AND PERSISTS ONLY WHEN RESISTED

SOCIETY DOESN'T GIVE US THE TIME & SPACE TO HEAL - WE HAVE TO TAKE IT

@simply_anxious

Daily Habit:

Prioritise your emotional wellbeing

Reframes to help you through the tough times...

When I learned that thoughts weren't facts and I actually have the power to rewire my brain, I was like, WOW! Why didn't someone tell me this sooner?

Those anxious thoughts that keep you stuck are just old, regurgitated data from your past experiences/memories. They are not facts. They feel real because you've allowed them to headspace to run the show.

Let's start reframing those thoughts and creating some new, empowering ones. Let's stop looking at our current situation and future through the eyes of our past.

Reframes work. Just keep practising and saying them with conviction.

Don't let anyone tell you otherwise - mental and emotional health is the foundation upon which everything else in your life is built. It's the compass that guides your thoughts, emotions, and actions. All other aspects of your life can suffer without a solid foundation of mental well-being. So please know that prioritising your mental health is not selfish; it is a fundamental act of self-care that allows you to cultivate inner peace, resilience, and fulfilment.

Remember, you are worth investing in, and nurturing your mental health is the greatest investment you can give yourself.

Daily Habit:

Do something that nourishes and nurtures your mind

Isn't it surprising? None of these lessons were part of my childhood curriculum. I've gathered this wisdom along the tumultuous journey of combating anxiety. Have you ever found yourself ensnared by concerns over things beyond your influence?

Much like myself, I'm willing to bet you have, especially when anxiety takes the reins. It can make us feel utterly powerless, but that's far from the truth.

During these moments, we often ruminate on things we can't change. We become captives to our anxious thoughts, weaving intricate tales of all the potential horrors that could occur. This only intensifies our anxiety, as if these imagined scenarios were unfolding before our eyes. It distorts our perception and cognition.

One of the most valuable lessons I gleaned on my path to recovery was the art of redirecting my focus towards the things I could genuinely influence, just like the things in the above visual. And here's the kicker: these are actions you can take control of, whether anxiety is lurking or not.

Shifting your attention toward what you can manage not only alleviates stress but also has a remarkable transformative effect. It's akin to a small inner voice whispering, "Yes, this situation is challenging, but let's figure out what I can do to make it a tad more manageable and soothe my emotions."

WHAT I CAN CONTROL

In the realm of thoughts, where the mind does roam, Find peace and solace; make this place your home. Release the grip on worries you can't sway; embrace what's yours to shape and brighten your day.

Let go of the burdens you cannot change. In the garden of control, let wisdom arrange. Tend to the blooms of hope, let them unfurl, Nurture your heart, let serenity swirl.

With each mindful breath, the storms will subside As the ripples of calm in your soul coincide. In the dance of control, a healthier mind will find The power to heal, uplift, and bind.

In the tapestry of life, threads woven with care, Focus on what's yours, and you'll find solace there. For in the things you can control, you'll see a path to a healthier mind, serene and free.

Emotional Health Reminders...

You are healing not broken

You won't always feel this way

Slow down & take your time

Be kind to yourself

Your needs matter

You are safe. You're going to be OK

@simply_anxious

Life can feel so overwhelming for many of us and for many reasons. So here's a gentle reminder to help soothe and comfort you through whatever you are going through.

Remember, you have so many opportunities ahead of you. Don't let the chaos of today cloud those glimmers of hope.

What's something nice you can do for yourself or gift yourself today?

Don't Forget!

@Simply_Anxious

It's easy to forget these things when anxiety floods you. So here's a reminder to help stop you from slipping down the rabbit hole of despair.

Anxiety is a discomfort that can quickly escalate into a distressing nightmare when fuelled by secondary fear. It is this secondary fear that gets us into a complete tangle.

What helped me avoid this was to remind myself of the facts by sticking little reminders around the place (my car dashboard, fridge, and a printout in my purse). They gave me comfort when I needed it.

Why not give it a try as you work through your recovery?

I found that recovering from anxiety entails much more than just confronting your fears. It involves looking closely at your life, particularly your relationships, surroundings, behaviours, and expectations, with a willingness to make necessary changes. If we don't eliminate the stressors and emotional burdens from our lives, it can significantly impede our recovery journey.

Only when I did this did I realise the many factors fuelling my distress daily and impacting my progress!

Here's what I learned:

- **Prioritising your well-being is key;** no relationship or job should jeopardise it.

- **You can't heal in chaos.** The notion that family bonds are unbreakable is a misconception. Healthy relationships should enrich, not complicate, your life.

- Straining to meet others' expectations is detrimental; your expectations may also need reviewing.
- **The past no longer exists, so let it go.**
- Impatience fuels anxiety.
- No one truly has everything figured out. If offered a quick fix to recover, **RUN!**
- There are no shortcuts or instant fixes, unfortunately.

What you label yourself as and say to yourself repeatedly becomes your reality.

Daily Habit:

If something feels heavy let it go.

ANXIETY RECOVERY
SELF-TALK

@Simply_Anxious

'Be kind to yourself' is not just a saying. It's a healer, soother, empowerer and recharger. It allows you to connect with yourself and learn to enjoy your own company. It shows you what a beaut of a human you are.

Positive self-talk is empowering because it fuels self-belief and self-confidence. We reinforce our sense of agency and capability when we engage in uplifting internal conversations. This internal encouragement is a source of motivation and resilience, enabling us to tackle challenges with a can-do attitude. It empowers us to set and pursue ambitious goals, knowing we possess the strength and positivity needed to overcome obstacles. Ultimately, positive self- talk transforms self-doubt into self-empowerment, fostering a mindset of growth and self-improvement.

Here are some of the benefits that I have found since practising positive self-talk:

1. It helps boost your self-esteem and self-worth. When you consistently remind yourself of your strengths, accomplishments, and abilities, you start to believe in yourself more, which can lead to greater self-confidence.

2. It can reduce stress and anxiety. When you replace negative thoughts with positive ones, you create a more optimistic and relaxed mindset. This can help you better cope with challenging situations and reduce the harmful effects of chronic stress.

3. It fosters resilience, allowing you to bounce back quickly from setbacks and failures. When you approach difficulties with a positive attitude, you're more likely to see them as opportunities for growth rather than insurmountable obstacles.

4. It can also enhance your relationships. When you feel better about yourself, you're more likely to interact with others positively and confidently, leading to more fulfilling connections.

5. It can boost your motivation and drive. When you use positive affirmations and self-encouragement, you'll likely stay committed to your goals and persevere through challenges.

6. It can help regulate your emotions. When you engage in self- compassion and positive affirmations, you can manage negative emotions more effectively and maintain emotional balance.

Ultimately, positive self-talk contributes to a greater sense of overall well-being and life satisfaction. It helps you cultivate a more positive outlook on life and a more optimistic perspective on the future. It's important to note that positive self-talk doesn't mean ignoring or denying the challenges and difficulties in life. It means approaching those challenges with a constructive and optimistic attitude.

Daily Habit:

Practice reframing negative self-talk into encouraging and empowering self-talk.

Examples:

I AM ENOUGH

I AM CAPABLE

I AM WORTHY

1 AM LOVED

I AM ...

I Can Help Me

In tough times, when life gets loud and thoughts get heavy, it can feel like everything's closing in, and hope is a distant memory. But in those moments of despair, when it seems like no one else can lend a hand and the road ahead is unclear, here's a simple truth: I'm here and can help me.

Inside each of us is a well of strength we often forget about in the daily chaos. In those dark moments, we can tap into this inner power and remind ourselves that we can navigate through the storms.

Take a moment to sit with your thoughts, reflect on the times you've faced challenging situations, fought inner battles, and gained wisdom. No matter how tough, every challenge shows your ability to endure, adapt, and overcome.

When the world feels cold and indifferent, warm yourself with self-compassion. Recall the times you've been there for others, showing kindness and empathy. If you could be a support for them, you can surely be your own guiding light in the darkest hours.

It's easy to fall into feeling like a victim, thinking you're helpless in tough situations. But deep down, you have the strength to challenge that idea. You're not stuck in your circumstances; you're more like a sculptor, shaping your destiny with every choice you make.

Use the tools that empower you: resilience, self-love, and the unshakable belief that, no matter how tough things get, you have the power to rise above it.

When times feel hard and scary, when hope seems distant, tell yourself, "I can help me." Take a step forward with each affirmation, knowing the power to overcome is right within you.

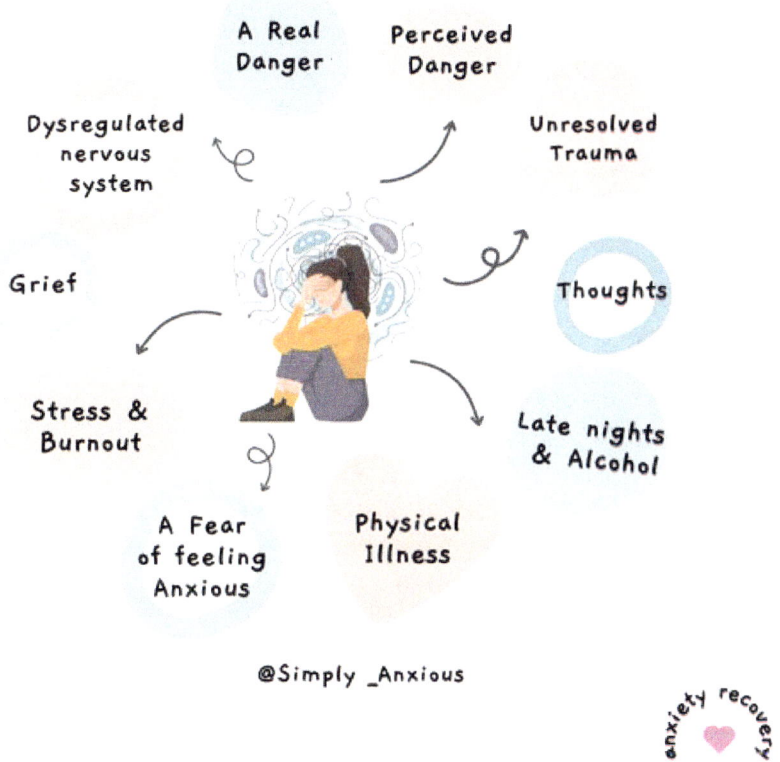

@Simply _Anxious

Labelling people struggling with anxiety and panic attacks as "mentally ill" does not help; I can speak from my own experience that this label added an extra burden to my already sensitised mind. A more accurate label could have been "emotionally distressed," coupled with a hopeful outlook like, "With time, space, and the right form of support, healing and recovery are achievable."

The terminology and words we use around anxiety hold significant weight. In my case, I wasn't grappling with "mental illness" (even though I experienced psychological symptoms like anxious and intrusive thoughts and DPDR).

I was experiencing emotional fatigue, mental exhaustion, and an overwhelmed and dysregulated nervous system, which naturally triggered anxiety. But for a long time, I didn't know this and so wore the 'I'm mentally ill' label, which I now know hindered my recovery.

And when I ditched this label and took the necessary time, space, and supportive guidance, I began to recover.

And you can, too.

Referring to oneself or being labelled as "mentally ill" doesn't help people struggling with anxiety.

Anxiety is a Symptom not an Illness

@Simply _Anxious

Here's a simple reminder for anyone who isn't feeling too good. It's okay, and the most important thing is that you don't have to worry about why you feel this way. You should take things slowly and be gentle with yourself.

I learned during my recovery that you don't always need a reason to feel a certain way. For example, if you feel anxious, it's okay to feel that way. The same goes for all emotions. Trying to make yourself feel something different from what you're feeling right now will only make you more stressed.

Please remember that all feelings and thoughts are temporary. They can't harm you or do what your mind might suggest. For many years, I thought my anxious feelings and thoughts would make me go crazy or worse, but they never did. They couldn't because they are just feelings and thoughts. They come and go faster when we don't attach meaning to them.

So, if you're not feeling great today, be kind to yourself and take it easy for now. Your body and mind will thank you for it. □

Keep an eye out for those little glimmers of hope, and hold onto them with all your might. Because hope:

> Illuminates your path and propels you toward your dreams.
> Fills you with the strength to endure.
> Transforms setbacks into stepping stones, making you bounce back even stronger!
> Infuses your days with a brighter mental and emotional state, bringing purpose and positivity into your life.
> It's not just for you; it's a gift that inspires others too!

Life has a way of sprinkling unexpected opportunities our way. Clinging to hope ensures that you're ready to embrace them.

So, let's keep hope burning brightly!

When you're anxious, those thoughts are not necessarily true because they often reflect your fears, worries, and insecurities rather than reality. Anxiety distorts our perception of events and situations, leading us to imagine all sorts of nonsense that is unlikely to happen or even impossible.

Anxious thoughts are based on past experiences or assumptions which don't reflect your current reality. For example, if you experienced anxiety while driving in the past, you may assume that if you drive on the same strip of the road, it will happen again, even if there is no evidence to support this.

So it's really important to remember that anxious thoughts are just thoughts, not truths. By challenging them, you can gain more confidence in your situation and reduce the anxiety.

Things I wish I'd known sooner about anxiety

- You are not damaged or less of a person if you struggle with anxiety
- Reframing thoughts helps shift their momentum away from fear
- Circumstances, environments & self-limiting beliefs can contribute to anxiety
- Focusing on soothing the nervous system is more beneficial than focusing on symptoms
- Anxiety will always pass, but a fear of it will prolong it
- You will always get through an anxiety storm, because anxiety cannot hurt you

We don't have to settle for less or put up with things that don't fulfil us. Often, though, that's precisely what we do. We endure way too many things, hoping they'll improve by themselves without taking action.

But we can start changing things today by taking small steps that can make a big difference in our lives.

Let's acknowledge the things that dim our light, drain and hold us back and start replacing them with things that inspire, encourage and support us.

Life's too short to...

- Live in fear
- Be around people who drain you!
- People please
- Believe you're not good enough
- Stay in a job, a relationship, a situation that crushes your spirit
- Remain stuck in the past

We don't have to settle for less or put up with things that don't fulfil us. Often, though, that's exactly what we do. We endure way too many things, hoping they'll improve by themselves without taking action.

But we can start changing things today by taking small steps that can make a big difference in our lives.

Let's acknowledge the things that dim, drain and hold us back and start replacing them with things that inspire, encourage and support us.

Let's get behind the wheel of our lives and start making those positive changes happen!

Anxiety Reminders

- anxiety is something you experience not who you are
- nothing is worth harming your emotional wellness & 'inner peace'
- anxious thoughts are perceived threats - not facts
- It's not about 'managing' anxiety. It's about healing, & reframing what's fuelling it
- it's the 'meaning' you give to something that makes it a 'trigger'
- you can't heal in chaos. You must distance yourself from it & give yourself some space

A turning point in my healing journey was learning how powerful beliefs are. At the start of my 'anxiety suffering,' a doctor told me that I could only ever "manage my anxiety," which I took to heart, essentially accepting that my condition was permanent. This belief became a driving force in my life, reshaping everything.

However, that changed when I discovered Dr Claire Weekes' book, 'Hope and Help for Your Nerves.' It gave me a new perspective, suggesting that I could recover from what I had come to see as a lifelong 'illness' I could only manage. From that point on, I embarked on a journey of recovery.

By believing that 'recovery was possible,' I completely shifted my mindset. The challenges I faced, the changes I made, and the discomfort I experienced all felt worthwhile because I now believed they would lead me to a place of healing. And indeed, they did. (it is not an overnight fix; it takes work, consistency and self-care).

This is my personal and truthful account of how I suffered for 20 years because I believed anxiety was an illness I could only ever 'manage'. And how stumbling across Dr Claire Weekes showed me the truth and a way out of that belief. 🙏

Find out more about Dr Claire Weekes at www.claireweekspublications.com

Contrary to what society has you believe these are probably the only things you need more of to feel content and at peace in your life.

It's a great guide for anxiety healing, too. 🙏

Anxiety recovery is filled with ups and downs, and that's okay. Take all the time and space you need; healing isn't about rushing but about healing and growth.

You're not alone and definitely NOT a burden; what you are is healing. Other people's frustration doesn't matter. What truly matters is YOU – your health, your well-being, and your recovery. So, let go of any guilt and focus on self-care. Reach out if you need support; it's a sign of strength, not weakness.

Let's help, support and uplift each other. Together, we break the anxiety stigma and heal as a compassionate community.

And to all those who haven't experienced anxiety: Please remember to BE KIND! Your understanding and empathy will create a much-needed safe space.

@simply_anxious

I am sending an abundance of love and compassion to anyone facing the challenges of anxiety. I truly understand how challenging it can be and want to affirm your experience.

It may sometimes feel overwhelming, but please know that recovery is possible. Please pay close attention to those small glimmers of hope and try to centre your focus on them instead of dwelling on the difficult moments. Acknowledge and take pride in the courage and strength that guide you on this journey. Grant yourself the patience and space necessary for healing, whatever that may look like.

You are deserving of this kindness, and always remember that you can overcome this.

SIGNS YOU'RE
SENSITISED

You've no energy

Your mind feels chaotic

You experience random waves of anxiety

You feel emotional & teary

Rest feels impossible

Everything feels like a stuggle

You feel like you're clinging to your sanity

Everything feels overwhelming

@Simply_Anxious

When you experience sensitisation, it's a clear sign that you need some valuable time and space to allow your nervous system to settle and find calmness. It's important to acknowledge that your system is currently overwhelmed, which is why you are going through this difficult experience.

If you don't have the time and space - make it and take it.

Behaviours that freed me from disordered anxiety

Spending time in nature, mindfulness

Practising staying with the feelings

challenging & reframing my thoughts

Reminding myself of the fACTS about anxiety

Speaking to myself with love

letting go of the self-limiting beliefs

Putting my mental wellbeing first

keeping things simple

Anxiety is a master at trickery with its symptoms. The main source of power over you is the anxious mind, which fools you into thinking you need to analyse, micromanage, have your safe person with you 24/7 and stay in your comfort zone to be safe. But the truth is you are safe without any of these things. This is how the anxious mind dictates your life and pulls all the strings.

Do you feel like this?

My recovery looked like...

Doing things no matter how I felt
Practising being comfortable with discomfort
Practising letting anxiety run its course
Seeing anxious moments as opportunities
Practising watching my thoughts
without identifying with them
Practising self-care and self-soothing
Not overcomplicating things
Distancing myself from drama
Adopting a 'I CAN' mindset
Speaking kind to myself

@simply_anxious

Feeling like you're not good enough is a tough place to be. But here's the truth: YOU ARE ENOUGH! Always have been always will be.

Don't let society's idea of "perfect" bring you down. Those perfect bodies and lifestyles are just marketing gimmicks designed to sell you stuff. And the opinions of others mean zilch. You don't need to change anything about yourself to be worthy of love, respect, and happiness. It's okay to work on yourself, but don't let self-improvement become a burden. You deserve to feel confident and capable just as you are.

So let's celebrate ourselves and each other. We don't need to be perfect to be awesome. We just need to be ourselves! □

Let's let go of the pressure to be or have something to feel complete. All that does is weigh us down and sometimes make life feel intolerable.

Your worth is not defined by others' opinions or society's expectations. When you embrace your true self and find peace in accepting who you are, the stress lifts and is replaced with joy.

How do I know? Because it's precisely what I'm experiencing now.

'I will be OK' because...

@Simply_Anxious

Choosing only the things that align with you is such a powerful and nurturing thing.

Life is a canvas, and you're the artist. Don't be afraid to paint it with your own colours, to the beat of your own drum. This is YOUR journey, and it's meant to be lived YOUR way.

I call these 'Life's little helpers' and are the things we often take for granted - the sunshine on our face, a glass of water when we're thirsty, a walk in nature. But these simple things can bring so much peace and help restore a sense of calm within us.

Let's take a moment to appreciate the small things in life and the way they support us on a daily basis. By acknowledging and embracing life's little helpers, we can find a deeper sense of gratitude and contentment in our lives.

So, whether it's a moment in the sun, a sip of cool water, or a walk in the park, let's say thank you to these simple yet powerful tools for wellbeing.

Quotes About Putting Yourself First

1. "You yourself, as much as anybody in the entire universe, deserve your love and affection." - Buddha

2. "Don't feel guilty for doing what's best for you." - Unknown

3. "Put yourself at the top of your to-do list every single day and the rest will fall into place." - Unknown

4. "You can't pour from an empty cup. Take care of yourself first." - Unknown

5. "Remember, you have been criticizing yourself for years and it hasn't worked. Try approving of yourself and see what happens." - Louise L. Hay

6. "Self-care is how you take your power back." - Lalah Delia

7. "Putting yourself first is not selfish. It's necessary." - Unknown

8. "You owe yourself the love that you so freely give to other people." - Unknown

9. "When you start taking care of yourself, you start feeling better, you start looking better, and you even start to attract better. It all starts with you." - Unknown

10. "Your relationship with yourself sets the tone for every other relationship you have." - Robert Holden

Remember that prioritising self-care and putting yourself first is essential for your well-being and can lead to healthier and more fulfilling relationships with others as well.

I'm mindful of how unkind the world can feel, especially now with rising costs and limited resources for support and care.

So, this post is for anyone currently finding life incredibly challenging. I want you to know that you truly matter; it won't always feel like this, and hope for a brighter future exists. 🙏

During any storm, it's important to reach out, share and seek support, and I want to share some avenues that may help.

How I became stuck
in the anxiety cycle

@simply_anxious

What helped me and can help you to break free from the anxiety cycle:

Give yourself some space and time
Practice self-soothing and grounding exercises
Don't feel pressured into things. Go at your own pace
Put yourself and your recovery FIRST
Connect with like-minded people
Stop labelling yourself and believing those thoughts
Get support - you don't have to do this alone
Support yourself with encouragement and compassion
Bin the idea that you are a burden. Because you are not!
Do the work!
Know that you will be OK

The truth is that the brightest smiles can hide the most profound struggles. Behind every successful, outgoing, kind, confident individual, there may be anxiety, fear, and intense exhaustion battling within.

Anxiety doesn't discriminate. It's not some illness that attacks only a few. Anxiety is in all of us. It plays a vital role in keeping us alive. And I believe the 'disorder bit' happens because of:

- our lack of understanding about what anxiety is,
- the conditioning that anything other than 'happy' means there's something wrong with you
- the lack of time and space society allows to process and heal difficult emotions
- the unrealistic expectations we are faced with daily

You're not damaged or doomed. You're exhausted and sensitised. And you're not alone in this.

So, let's break the stigma and create a space of understanding and compassion where we uplift and support one another, regardless of what lies beneath the surface.

Anxiety doesn't mean you are weak! I love this. It's a great reminder that even if you have anxiety, it doesn't make you less of a person. It's also more accurate to say that you're a person whose nervous system has become overwhelmed and sensitised by life's experiences.

Labels are for Products, not people!

Quotes About Courage and Healing

1. "Healing takes courage, and we all have courage, even if we have to dig a little to find it." - Tori Amos

2. "The wound is the place where the light enters you." - Rumi

3. "Courage doesn't happen when you have all the answers. It happens when you are ready to face the questions you have been avoiding your whole life." - Shannon L. Alder

4. "It takes courage to grow up and become who you really are." - E.E. Cummings

5. "You have within you right now, everything you need to deal with whatever the world can throw at you." - Brian Tracy

6. "The beautiful thing about fear is, when you run to it, it runs away." - Robin Sharma

7. "You gain strength, courage, and confidence by every experience in which you really stop to look fear in the face. You are able to say to yourself, 'I lived through this horror. I can take the next thing that comes along.'" - Eleanor Roosevelt

8. "Healing may not be so much about getting better, as about letting go of everything that isn't you – all of the expectations, all of the beliefs – and becoming who you are." - Rachel Naomi Remen

9. "It's okay to be scared. Being scared means you're about to do something really, really brave." - Mandy Hale

Healing Anxiety Instead of...

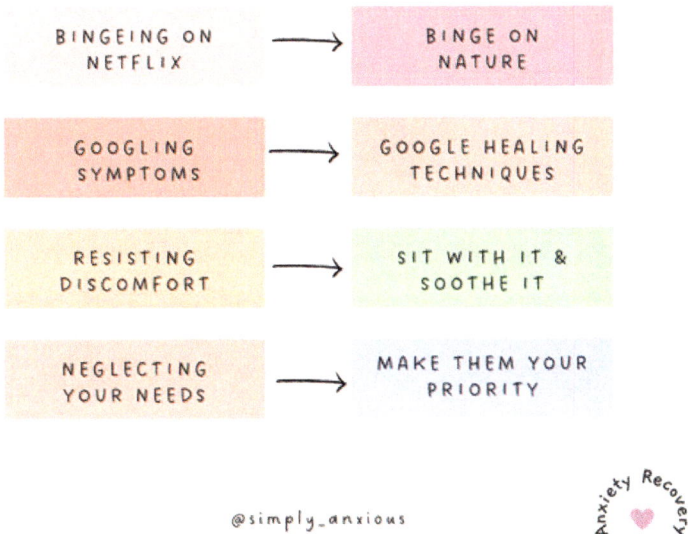

Let's take a moment to breathe, reflect, and choose things that bring us peace instead of adding to our anxiety.

It could be listening to an inspiring podcast, exploring nature's beauty on a simple walk, or simply savouring a warm cup of tea while watching the sunset.

Engaging in things like painting, journaling, or gardening can also be incredibly therapeutic.

Remember, there's no rush. Let's slow down, tune into ourselves, and prioritise the stuff that nourishes our soul and find solace in the things that reduce anxiety rather than exacerbate it.

It's easy to forget these things when anxiety floods us. So here's a little reminder to help prevent you from slipping down the rabbit hole of despair.

Anxiety is a discomfort that can quickly escalate into a distressing nightmare when fuelled by secondary fear. It is this secondary fear that prolongs the suffering.

What helped me avoid this was to remind myself of the facts - I had little reminders stuck around the place (car dashboard, fridge, a printout in my purse), which brought comfort when I needed it. Why not give it a try as you work through your recovery?

Anxiety Recovery

things that matter	things that don't
going at your own pace	other people's expectations
taking consistant small steps	taking big steps
nourishing yourself with inspiring content	being perfect
gently encouraging yourself	how quickly you recover
being patient with yourself	letting people down
being kind & caring to yourself	what people think of you

In my healing journey, I realised the things that truly matter and those that simply don't.

Anxiety can cloud our judgment and amplify our worries, making it challenging to focus on what really deserves our attention and energy.

So please remember, there will be so many things that don't deserve your attention as you heal anxiety. So focus your energy only on what truly matters, and watch your healing journey bloom.

If all you keep telling yourself, is I can't, I'm scared, and I'm not enough, that is how you will feel. It took me so long to realise this!

Practising reframing thoughts isn't a gimmick. It really does help because our thoughts are linked to our feelings and behaviours.

We think we can't do something because we repeatedly tell ourselves that we can't. But unfortunately, we do this so often that self-limiting thoughts become a regular part of our reality.

But they don't need to, and we can learn to stop them through reframing.

I used to fill my days with the things I've listed on the left, thinking they would speed up my recovery. But you know what? They only added to my stress and kept me in a never-ending anxiety loop.

From my own journey, I want to remind you that it's okay to let go of behaviours that don't serve you. Instead, focus on what truly matters – your needs, healing, and overall well-being.

Reach out to those who understand and will validate your feelings. Let go of the pressure to recover quickly and embrace your own unique pace. Don't let society's expectations dictate your healing journey – trust in the process.

Believe me, once I made these changes, life started feeling lighter, and I began to heal.

Embracing what truly resonates with you is a profoundly empowering and nurturing choice. Picture life as a canvas awaiting your artistic touch. Fearlessly splash it with the vibrant hues of your own choosing, marching to the rhythm of your unique melody. This journey is exclusively yours, intended to be experienced on your terms.

Quotes About Safety

1. "Safety is not the absence of danger, but the presence of courage in the face of it." - Unknown
2. "In the storm of anxious thoughts, find solace in the sanctuary of your own strength. You are safer than your fears would have you believe." - Anonymous
3. "Amidst the chaos of the anxious mind, remember: your safety is not a question mark but a steadfast truth, grounded in the present moment." - Author Unknown
4. "Fear may knock on the door of your mind, but only courage will answer. Your safety is in the resilience that resides within you." - Anonymous
5. "The anxious mind weaves tales of uncertainty, but the heart whispers a truth: you are safe in the haven of your own existence." - Unknown
6. "Trust the whispers of your inner strength when anxiety screams doubt. Your safety is not negotiable; it is a constant companion within." - Anonymous
7. "Anxiety may cast shadows, but you are the bearer of an unwavering light called resilience. In its glow, safety is an undeniable reality." - Author Unknown
8. "Even when the anxious mind spins tales of peril, the fortress of your inner calm stands unshaken. Safety is your birthright, not a fleeting illusion." - Anonymous
9. "The anxious mind is a storyteller, but you hold the pen to your narrative. In every chapter, inscribe the truth: you are safe, you are resilient." - Unknown

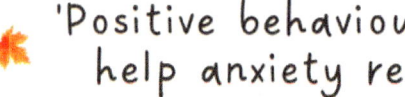

A little reminder of some of the changes you can make to support your recovery.

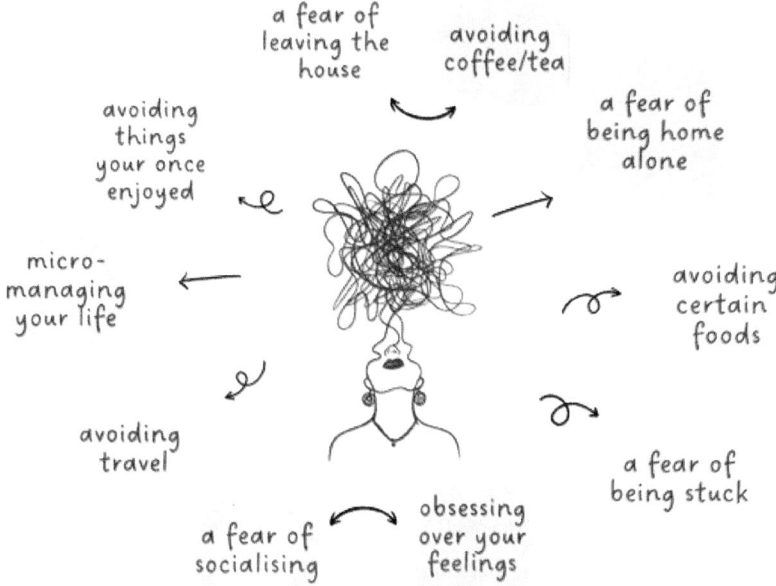

When I realised, it was a fear of feeling anxious that was at the core of my avoidance behaviours and belief in my anxious mind's stories. I was able to work solely on that fear and change my relationship with anxiety. Before this, I had what felt like a million triggers I had to deal with. But the truth was it was only one. The fear of feeling anxious in any given situation because I believed that anxiety could hurt me.

Do you have any of these fears? And if I could wave a magic wand and tell you you'd never feel anxious again, would you still avoid/do these things?

BE AROUND PEOPLE WHO...

@Simply_anxious

Who we spend our time with matters, especially when healing anxiety.

So please don't be afraid to spring-clean your friends' list; keep family members who discourage you at arm's length and distance yourself from anyone who tries to dim your light. You don't need them.

Instead, spend time with people who do value you, lift you up and help you to shine.

Anxiety at times of celebration (birthdays, Christmas etc.)

Navigating any period of celebration can be both fun and stressful. If you're struggling with anxiety, though, consider trying these soothing ideas to help create a more calming and enjoyable experience:

1. Mindful Breathing: Practice deep, mindful breathing exercises to help calm your nervous system. Focus on your breath, inhaling slowly and deeply, then exhaling with intention. This simple technique can be done anywhere and at any time.

2. Create a Cosy Space: Designate a comfortable and calming space in your home. Decorate it with soft blankets, pillows, and warm lighting. Having a comfy space can provide a sense of security and peace.

3. Nature Walks: Take advantage of the calming influence of walks in nature. Whether it's a stroll in a nearby park or a hike in the woods, spending time outdoors can restore and help clear your mind.

4. Warm Beverages: Treat yourself to warm, comforting beverages like herbal tea, hot chocolate, and soups. Sipping a warm drink can be soothing and provide a moment of relaxation.

5. Aromatherapy: Experiment with calming scents such as lavender, chamomile, or vanilla. Whether through essential oils, candles, or incense, aromatherapy can positively influence your mood and reduce anxiety.

6. Mindful Coloring: Engage in mindful colouring or drawing to redirect your focus and promote relaxation. There are many adult colouring books designed specifically for stress relief that you can explore.

7. Digital Detox: Take breaks from your phone and social media. Limiting screen time can help reduce the constant stream of information and potential stressors, allowing your mind to unwind.

8. Express Gratitude: Use the time as a time for reflection. Consider starting a gratitude journal, jotting down things you're thankful for each day. Focusing on positive aspects of your life can shift your mindset and alleviate anxiety.

9. Gentle Exercise: Engage in gentle exercises like yoga or tai chi. These practices not only benefit your physical health but also promote mental well-being through mindful movement and stretching.

10. Reading or Listening to Soothing Music: Escape into a good book or listen to calming music. Create a playlist of your favourite soothing tunes to have on hand when you need a moment of tranquillity.

11. Set Realistic Expectations: Manage expectations for the holiday season by setting realistic goals. It's okay not to do everything— prioritise what truly matters and allow yourself to enjoy the festivities at your own pace.

12. Connect with Loved Ones: Reach out to friends or family members for support and connection. Sharing your thoughts and feelings can provide comfort and remind you that you're not alone.

Remember that self-care is a personal journey and finding what works best for you is essential. Incorporating these soothing ideas into your daily routine can contribute to more peaceful and enjoyable holiday and celebratory times.

One of the challenging things about dealing with anxiety is those endless loops of overthinking.

When we are sensitised, our minds get way too chatty with worries and what-ifs. When we identify with these thoughts, they can go overboard. Remember, just because you think something doesn't mean it's true. Overthinking won't necessarily keep you safe and can make you feel more anxious.

Here are some mini habits to do instead:

1. **Challenge Your Thoughts:** ask, "Is this thought based on facts, or is it an automatic thought pattern?" remind yourself that you're capable and safe.

2. **Distract Yourself:** Do something you enjoy, exercise, or listen to an inspiring podcast. This can help shift your focus away from overthinking.

3. **Talk it out:** Sometimes, just talking about it can make you feel better and give you a fresh perspective.

Remember, it's normal to have anxious thoughts, but you can choose whether or not to let them control you. You've got the power to manage your mind and reduce overthinking.

How Anxiety impacted me

my mind
Made me feel like I was going crazy & losing control with the DPDR, low self-belief, anxious & intrusive thoughts & feel ununsafe

my body
Made me feel like I was sick with horrendous symptoms like- palpitations, shortness of breath, tight throat, headaches etc

my behaviour
Made me avoid, overthink, doubt, obsess about things, develop unhealthy habits, talk to myself in a negative way

my life
It shrank my world, restricted my enjoyment, held me hostage, stole my zest for life, doomed

@Simply_Anxious

I wouldn't wish disordered anxiety on anyone. But unfortunately, it's something that impacts the lives of many in today's world.

If you're suffering, please be kind to yourself, reach out for support, slow down and take all the time you need to heal & recover. You will be ok!

Oh, and get yourself a copy of Dr Claire Weekes's Hope & Help for your Nerves book. It can change your life.

Don't let daily habits overwhelm you. Life is too short for unnecessary hardships. Here are quick reminders:

>You're enough as you are.

>You're stronger than you realize.

>Be yourself and speak your truth.

>Your feelings are valid.

Don't live in fear or restrict yourself for others. Embrace your true self and let go of unnecessary worries.

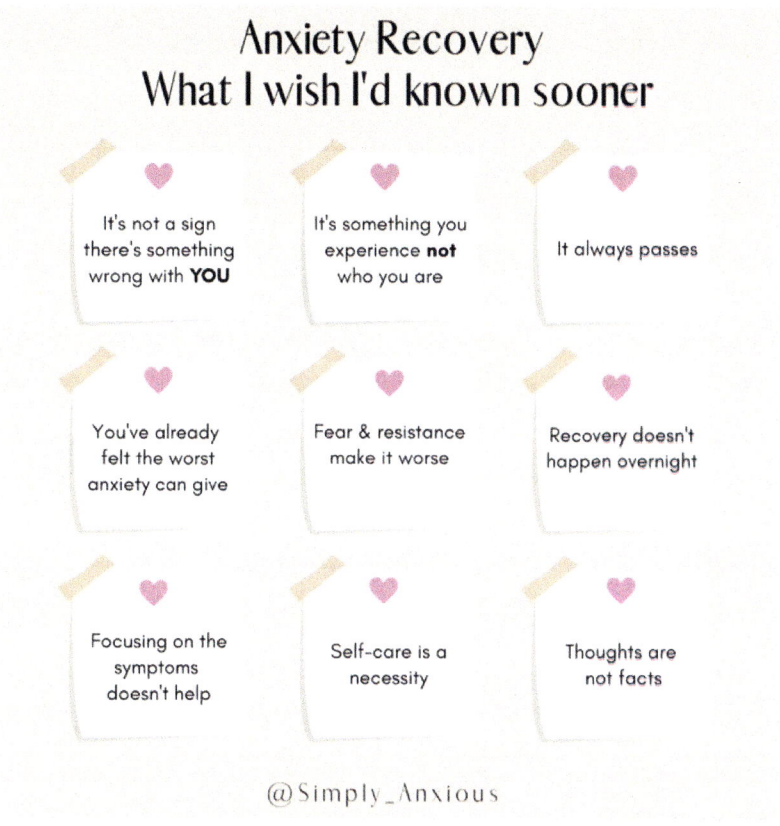

If I had known these things sooner, I believe I wouldn't have suffered for as long as I did. But I didn't; instead, I wasted years innocently doing things that fuelled the anxiety and kept me in an anxious cycle.

> Labelling myself as an anxious person made me feel damaged.
>
> Being told I couldn't recover left me feeling defeated
>
> Trying to eliminate symptoms just turned into something similar to a game of whack-a-mole.
>
> My impatience to recover (once I knew I could) just added stress and feelings of shame.

If only I'd been given facts and the proper support all those years ago, anxiety would have still felt horrid, but the secondary fear leading to years of suffering would have had no basis for growth.

The gift in all of this is my now-lived experience, something I can share in the hope that others don't make the same mistakes I did.

Here are some things that can help stop secondary fear:

1. **Mindful Awareness:** Cultivate awareness of your thoughts and recognize when secondary fears emerge. Mindfulness allows you to observe thoughts without judgment, helping to prevent the escalation of anxiety.

2. **Challenge Negative Thoughts:** Actively challenge and reframe negative thoughts. Question the validity of the secondary fears and consider alternative, more rational perspectives to reduce their impact on your anxiety.

3. **Focus on the Present Moment:** Ground yourself in the present moment. Anxiety often thrives on anticipation of future events. By staying present, you can reduce the influence of hypothetical fears that may contribute to anxiety.

4. **Limit Information Intake:** Avoid excessive exposure to negative news or information that may fuel secondary fears. Selectively choose what information you consume, and ensure it comes from reliable sources to maintain a balanced perspective.

5. **Establish Healthy Coping Mechanisms:** Develop healthy coping mechanisms. This could include activities like exercise, deep breathing, or engaging in hobbies that bring joy, helping to counteract the impact of secondary fears.

6. **Seek Support:** Talk to friends, family, or a mental health professional. Sharing your thoughts and fears can provide valuable perspectives, preventing the buildup of secondary fears that may exacerbate anxiety.

DAILY HABITS
TO SOOTH ANXIETY

@SIMPLY_ANXIOUS

Learning to accept and work through anxiety takes time. So, to help you practice, here are some ways I'd calm and soothe my anxiety symptoms when they felt too much.

They may seem simple, but they are incredibly effective - trust me.

There's no getting away from it - mental health is the foundation upon which everything else in your life is built. It's the compass that guides your thoughts, emotions, and actions. Without a solid foundation of mental well-being, all other aspects of your life can suffer. So please know that prioritising your mental health is not selfish; it is a fundamental act of self-care that allows you to cultivate inner peace, resilience, and fulfilment.

Remember, you are worth investing in, and nurturing your mental health is the greatest investment you can give yourself.

'Mini' Habits to beat anxiety for healing

@Simply_Anxious

Here are a few healthy habits to consider that will benefit your healing journey. And your mind will absolutely love.

One of the main behaviours that trap us in an unending cycle of anxiety is the interpretation we attach to our anxious feelings and the meaning we give them.

Our excessive worry about anxiety tends to exacerbate it, setting off a relentless loop of negativity. Fear begets worry, and worry, in turn, fuels the flames of anxiety.

The solution is surprisingly simple. Instead of harshly judging how we feel when anxious, we can acknowledge it compassionately and concentrate on supporting ourselves during these moments.

Use this week too...

LET GO
focus on what you want & not on what you don't want

SLOW DOWN
whatever you have to do, do it at your own pace

TRUST
look at 'what could go right' not 'what could go wrong'

EMPOWER
you've got through every challenge and will continue to

BELIEVE
you can do hard things, you are capable you prove this daily

BE PATIENT
acknowledge that healing takes time. Accept this and ease your stress

This week, let's courageously step into the unknown and use the opportunity to challenge ourselves, expand our comfort zones, and discover hidden strengths we may not have realised we have.

By embracing new things, we can begin to cultivate a deep sense of self-belief, recognising our resilience and inner strength. So let's shift our defeatest mindset and instead remind ourselves of our worth and capabilities, soothe our fears with self-assurance and blossom with every new step we take.

See this week as an opportunity to change and empower yourself. Ask for support if you haven't already and connect with others who will cheer you on. You can do hard things. You prove that every day.

Use this week to recognise and celebrate that!

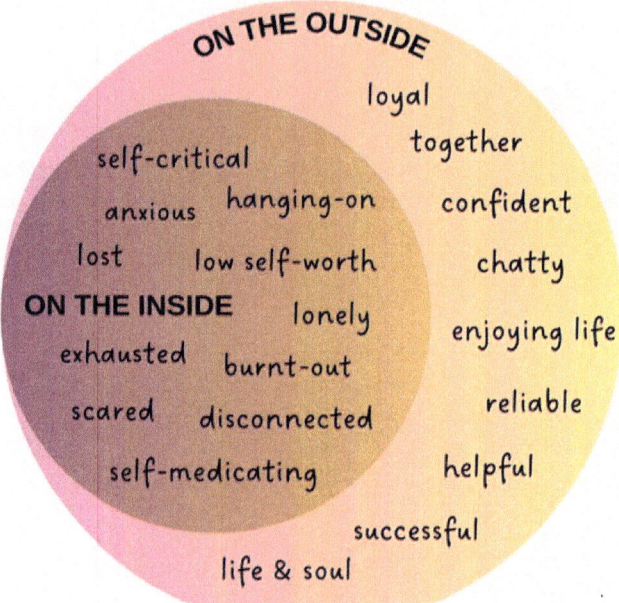

The truth is that the brightest smiles can hide the deepest struggles. Behind every successful, outgoing, kind, confident individual, there may be anxiety, fear, and emotional fatigue battling within.

Anxiety doesn't discriminate. It's not some illness that attacks only a few. Anxiety is in all of us. It plays a vital role in keeping us alive. And I believe the 'disorder bit' happens because of our lack of understanding about anxiety, the conditioning that anything other than 'happy' means there's something wrong with you. The lack of time and space in society to process and heal difficult emotions and the unrealistic expectations we are faced with daily

You're not damaged or doomed. You're exhausted and sensitised. And you're not alone in this.

OUTSIDE THE COMFORT ZONE

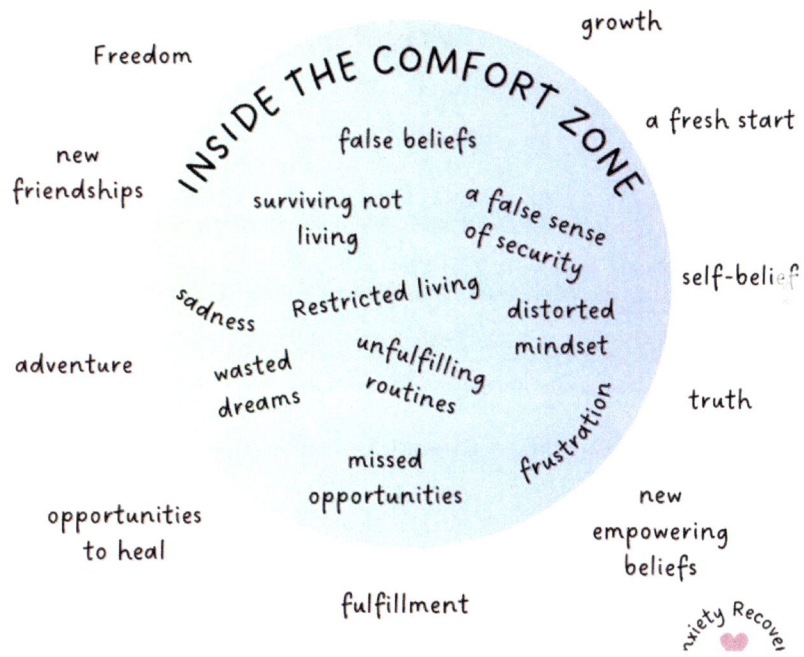

Stepping outside of your comfort zone can feel scary, but it's where growth and healing happen.

We see its magic when we embrace it with curiosity and adventure and take small steps. The truth is you're capable of more than you realise, and outside of your comfort zone, you will witness this.

When you make 'You' your comfort zone, you'll be free to do anything, go anywhere and always feel safe and at home.

Baby steps.

BE AROUND PEOPLE WHO...

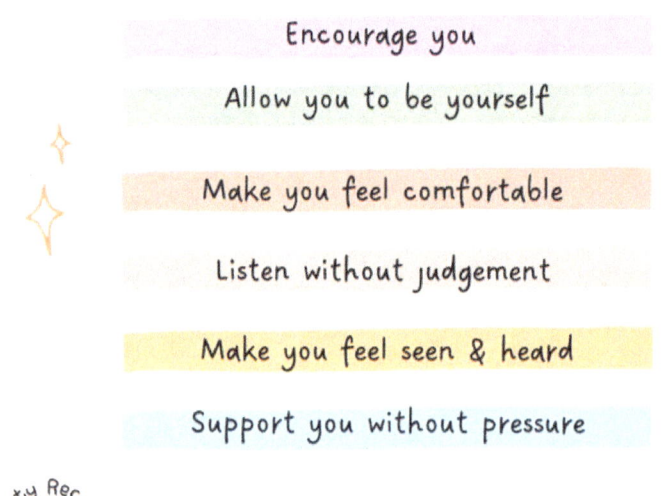

Encourage you

Allow you to be yourself

Make you feel comfortable

Listen without judgement

Make you feel seen & heard

Support you without pressure

Who we spend our time with matters, especially when healing anxiety.

So please don't be afraid to spring-clean your friends' list; keep family members who discourage you at arm's length and distance yourself from anyone who tries to dim your light. You don't need them. Set some boundaries to help protect your peace.

Instead, spend time with people who do value you, lift you and help you to shine

A letter to myself

I hope this letter gives you peace amidst the challenges and uncertainties that may cloud your mind. I want you to know that you are not alone, and even in the darkest moments, a glimmer of light is waiting to guide you.

Life can be tough, and I understand that you may be facing difficulties that seem insurmountable right now. It's okay to feel overwhelmed, to question, and to doubt. However, I want to remind you that you are stronger than you think, more resilient than you realise, and capable of overcoming whatever comes your way.

In the storm of life, it may be hard to see beyond the clouds, but trust me, the sun is still shining above them. This, too, shall pass, and as the days unfold, you will find strength and courage within yourself that you never knew existed.

Remember that it's okay to lean on others for support. You are not alone in this struggle. Friends, family, and even those you may not expect are ready to lend a helping hand or a listening ear. Don't hesitate to reach out, share your burdens, and let others share in your journey.

In moments of despair, could you reflect on the journey you've been able to travel so far? You've faced challenges before and emerge stronger and wiser each time. This time will be no different. Embrace the lessons, no matter how difficult, for they shape you into a more resilient and compassionate person.

Give yourself the grace to feel and the space to heal. It's okay to take one step at a time, even if the path ahead seems long and hard. You have the strength within you to endure, to persevere, and to rise above.

Believe in yourself, as I believe in you. The road may be challenging, but you are capable. Be patient with yourself, and trust that, in time, things will get better. This struggle is just one chapter of your life, not the whole story.

You are capable, you are strong, and you are not alone. Take a deep breath, face the challenges with courage, and know that brighter days are ahead. It's going to be okay.

I believe in you,

Love yourself

A healing exercise is to write a letter to yourself full of encouragement and love - give it a try!

Does this resonate? For years, I felt like this. I was desperate to recover but too scared to take the steps needed. I knew what I needed to do, but I was afraid because of thoughts/beliefs like these dominating my mind. Let's be truthful. Anticipatory anxiety is hard!

Change is scary, but the thought of another ten years living under the restrictions that my fear of anxiety had created was terrifying. So, with that in mind, I was willing to endure whatever discomfort came up while recovering, knowing it would be temporary. I had nothing to lose and my freedom to gain! I also want to reassure you if you have fears like these None of these 'fears' ever happened.

ANXIETY AT NIGHT
feels like...

- You're all alone in the world suffering, and no one can help you
- The worst anxiety you've ever felt
- Your brain is in overdrive with racing, fearful thoughts
- You've been woken by a jolt of pure terror and unease
- Every cell in your body is wired with fear

@simply_anxious

Have you ever experienced panic at night?

Nothing is worse than waking to a gripping "feeling" of fear soaked to the skin in sweat and trembling. The anxiety feels much more amplified in the still of the night, leaving us feeling scared and isolated.

Daytime provides distractions from anxious thoughts. We can try to busy ourselves to escape anxiety. But at night, there are no distractions as you lie in bed. Also, anxiety can worsen at night due to tiredness, making it more challenging to cope and positively deal with our anxious thoughts.

What helped me with night panic while recovering was:

- Exercising at least once daily and practising breathing techniques. This helped burn off any negative energy and helped to calm my nervous system. I would also quickly walk around the block an hour before bed.
- Dimming the lights 30 minutes before bed, listening to soothing music or a calming podcast, and drinking chamomile tea.
- Cut out caffeine and alcohol (I'm alcohol-free nowadays, which I wish I'd done years ago), and take a natural supplement (like Kalms) to help me fall asleep faster and get better sleep!
- When the panic set in, instead of lying-in bed worrying, I'd get up and do something else, e.g. I'd wash my face with cold water and then read for a bit. Or listen to nature sounds, do a guided meditation, or journal to clear my head. Although anxiety at night can feel distressing, it is essential not to add more fear. Instead, try to be as self-soothing as possible and remind yourself that it will pass.

Remember you are safe.

How Anxiety Fatigue *Feels*

Being subjected to prolonged periods of anxiety can lead to nervous fatigue. So, then we have two problems.

1. Our fear of anxiety and 2. The effects that fear has on our emotional and physical health. Anxiety is only supposed to be a short-term response to save us from danger. Not something that releases a continuous torrent of stress hormones to save us from the threat that is only alive in our thoughts.

But that is what happens when we develop a fear of anxiety. Anxiety doesn't make us sick. Instead, the continuous flow of stress hormones, mental fatigue, and exhaustion make us sick, which only occurs from our fear of anxiety. To help us out of this awful cycle, we must start practising self-care and distancing ourselves from our thoughts.

Learning to accept that if the 'danger' isn't right there in the present moment, it doesn't exist, and we do not have to worry ourselves sick over it. Acknowledging that the sensations and symptoms result from the stress hormones, they can't hurt us. It will ease once we refrain from using anxiety-fueling behaviours, e.g. trying to think our way out of anxiety, trying to fix ourselves, trying to avoid our feelings, and trying to be safe from a threat that doesn't exist. It is all the 'trying' that's causing us to suffer.

Instead, focus on what you want, not what you don't want. And work on that. e.g. I want to feel calm and anxiety-free. Practice self-care, learn to soothe and ground yourself, and gradually challenge yourself away from your fear of anxiety via gentle exposure. It's how I eventually recovered by changing my behaviours and beliefs around anxiety, accepting it as a harmless albeit intense emotional discomfort and not as a life or sanity-threatening illness that my thoughts tried to convince me it is.

ANXIETY SYMPTOMS
THAT MADE ME THINK I WAS LOSING MY MIND

01 ZONING OUT
02 FEELING LIKE I WAS IN A DREAM
03 EMOTIONAL NUMBNESS
04 FEELING DISCONNECTED
05 FEELING INTENSE ANGER
06 STRUGGLING TO REMEMBER STUFF
07 UNABLE TO CONCENTRATE
08 INTRUSIVE THOUGHTS

Simply_Anxious

I used to be really scared of specific anxiety symptoms, especially when they made me feel like I was losing touch with reality. It was my biggest fear.

My dad told me that people who actually lose touch with reality don't realise it's happening. So, the fact that I could feel afraid and ask myself if I'm going 'crazy' meant that I probably wasn't. Knowing this from my dad made a big difference.

Even though anxiety might make it seem like you're going crazy, it's actually a common reaction to a surge of adrenaline, which happens during high anxiety and panic.

I found this out when I read about anxiety symptoms. But weirdly, it's not talked about much, even though many people go through it. If you're worried about this, know you're not alone.

I also want to share that, even though I often felt like I had no control over this feeling, when the anxiety calmed down, these symptoms went away. Plus, even though I was scared of losing control and being out of touch with reality for more than ten years, it never actually happened. I hope this brings some comfort.

ANXIETY

I'm not faking being ill.
I'm actually faking being well...

@simply_anxious

A gentle reminder: It's absolutely okay not to be okay.

The quote in this illustration resonates deeply with me as it mirrored my own life for years.

Societal stigma and a distorted perception of humanity often leads us to conceal our mental and emotional struggles. It's time to acknowledge that these should be embraced, just like physical health. Thanks to advocates and voices speaking out, society is gradually recognising that the brain, like any other organ, can face challenges.

Don't burden yourself with the pressure to appear okay when you're not. There's no shame in admitting you're struggling; many more people than you realise are too. And help is available.

Anxiety can be profoundly distressing, overshadowing one's true self. It's okay to acknowledge its impact and not pretend everything is fine.

Putting your energy into appearing 'normal' is exhausting and could be better used for healing. You have nothing to feel ashamed of.

Let's release any shame we may feel, openly discuss our struggles, and contribute to breaking the stigma around mental health. Remember, everyone has mental health, making everyone susceptible to challenges.

So, let's take thew weight off our shoulders and normalise this!

Please remember that you have got through everything you thought you couldn't and today is a new day where we get to acknowledge that, feel proud and shower ourselves with compassion.

Some of us will be wrapped in cotton wool feeling emotionally fragile today. But please remember it will be ok. These emotional storms are temporary and brighter days are most certainly ahead. Don't ever forget that!

How to Build Your Inner Strength

Building inner strength is a gradual and intentional process involving resilience, self-awareness, and a positive mindset. Here are some ways to help you build and nurture your inner strength that helped me:

Cultivate Self-Awareness:
Start by understanding yourself better. Reflect on your values, strengths, and areas for growth. Journaling, meditation, and regular self-reflection can help with self-awareness.

Set Realistic Goals:
Break down your larger goals into smaller, achievable steps. Celebrate your accomplishments along the way, as achieving even small steps contributes to a sense of competence and inner strength.

Face Challenges Positively:
Embrace challenges as opportunities for growth rather than insurmountable obstacles. Adopt a positive mindset and view setbacks as learning experiences to build resilience.

Develop Healthy Coping Mechanisms:
Identify and cultivate healthy ways to cope with stress and adversity. This could include deep breathing, mindfulness, exercise, or engaging in hobbies that bring you joy.

Establish and Maintain Boundaries:
Learn to set boundaries in your personal and professional life. Communicate your limits and prioritise self-care. Knowing when to say "no" is crucial to building inner strength. And don't feel guilty about it.

Practice Gratitude:
Cultivate a gratitude mindset by focusing on the positive aspects of your life. Regularly acknowledge and appreciate the good things, no

matter how small, to foster resilience and inner well-being.

Build a Support System:
Surround yourself with positive and supportive individuals. Share your thoughts and feelings with those you trust. A strong support system can provide encouragement during challenging times.

Embrace Change:
Develop adaptability by embracing change as a natural part of life. Recognise that flexibility and openness to new experiences contribute to your ability to navigate life's twists and turns.

Face Fears Gradually:
Challenge yourself to step out of your comfort zone. Facing fears gradually, in a controlled manner, can build confidence and inner strength. Each small victory contributes to your overall resilience.

Keep Learning:
Stay curious and open to learning new things. This can enhance your sense of competence and self-efficacy, fostering a belief in your ability to overcome challenges.

Express Yourself Creatively:
Engage in creative outlets that allow you to express your emotions. Whether through art, writing, music, or other forms of creativity, self-expression can be a powerful tool for building inner strength.

Practice Self-Compassion:
Be kind to yourself. Acknowledge that everyone faces difficulties, and treat yourself with the same compassion you would offer to a friend. Self-compassion is a key component of inner strength.

Please be patient and remember that building inner strength is a continuous process, and it's okay to progress at your own pace. Be patient with yourself, celebrate your successes, and learn from your challenges. Over time, you'll find that your inner strength grows, helping you navigate life with resilience and grace.

YOU ARE ARE STRONGER THAN YOU THINK

Finding Hope

I want to tell you something important, especially if you're feeling really overwhelmed by anxiety. It might seem like things won't get better, but I promise you, they will.

Imagine your life like a giant storybook. Anxiety feels like a tricky part of the story right now, but it's not the whole story. It's just one chapter, a chapter that can change and lead to better days.

You're actually really strong, even if it doesn't feel like it. The fact that you're dealing with anxiety shows how tough you are. And you don't have to face it alone. There are people who care about you and will want to help. Share your feelings with them, and you might find it easier when you're not facing everything alone. There are also online groups for people where a community heal together.

Life has ups and downs. Sometimes, it feels rough, but those tough times won't last forever. Just like clouds that move away, your anxious feelings will also pass, making room for calmer and happier moments.

Remember, healing takes time. It's like a slow and steady journey, not a race. Don't forget to celebrate the small victories. Those little wins will add up to a future where anxiety has less control over your feelings. Be patient with yourself, and don't rush the process.

Believe that you can get better and recover. Even though your mind may feel tangled up with worries right now, your mind can also imagine a future where you feel more peaceful. Practice visualising that. Treat yourself kindly, like you would a good friend. Picture a life where anxiety doesn't have such a strong hold on you.

So, my friend, as you go through these tough feelings, know you'll be okay. The way to feeling better might be a bit twisted, but each step brings you closer to a brighter and more hopeful tomorrow. Trust in your strength, lean on the people who care about and understand you, and remember, this chapter of anxiety is just a small part of your story. There are brighter days ahead.

Much Love,

Lisa x

Embracing Slow Healing

In the hustle and bustle of our fast-paced lives, slowing down may seem impossible. Yet, when it comes to emotional healing, taking things slow can be a powerful and transformative approach. Just like a delicate flower needs time to bloom, our emotional wounds require patience and gentle care.

The Rushing Dilemma
The unspoken pressure to quickly heal, get better challenges, and move on isn't helpful. We're encouraged to "get over it" or "bounce back" swiftly. However, emotions don't always conform to our timelines. Imagine a broken bone – you wouldn't rush the healing process; the same principle applies to emotional wounds.

Understanding Emotional Healing
Emotional healing is not a linear journey; it's a process filled with twists, turns, and moments of reflection. It's about acknowledging the pain, allowing ourselves to feel it, and gradually working through the layers of emotions. By taking things slow, we grant ourselves the space needed for genuine healing to unfold.

Honouring Your Emotions
When we rush through the healing process, we risk suppressing our emotions rather than addressing them. We patch over them, which doesn't work in the long term. Taking things slow means giving yourself permission to feel the pain, anger, or sadness. These emotions are not weaknesses; they are stepping stones towards better health and

healing.

Building a Strong Foundation
Think of emotional healing as constructing a building. Each brick represents a step in the healing process. Rushing through these steps might lead to an unstable structure but taking the time to carefully lay each brick ensures a solid foundation for lasting recovery.

Learning and Growing
Emotional healing is not just about moving past the pain; it's an opportunity for profound personal growth. By taking things slow, you allow yourself the chance to learn from your experiences and gain valuable insights that will contribute to your emotional resilience.

Cultivating Self-Compassion
Taking things slow is an act of self-compassion. It's about treating yourself with the same kindness and understanding you would offer to a friend. Rushing the healing process can lead to self-judgment and unrealistic expectations. Embrace the gentleness of time, allowing yourself to heal at your own pace.

Nurturing Connections
Slow healing also extends to the relationships around you. When you take the time to heal, you create space for genuine connections with others. Communicate your needs and boundaries, allowing those around you to offer support in a way that aligns with your healing journey.

Embrace the Journey
In today's society, the art of slow healing may seem unconventional. However, the depth of emotional healing requires time, understanding, and self-compassion. Embrace the journey, savour the moments of growth, and let the healing unfold naturally. Society can wait! Your wellbeing can't.

I Will Leave You With This - A Glimmer of Hope

To the weary heart battling the storm of anxiety, I offer you these words as a gentle breeze of hope. In the darkest corners of your mind, where anxious thoughts loom, it may feel like the sun will never break through the clouds. But let me assure you, my friend, that even the stormiest nights eventually surrender to dawn's tender light.

Anxiety is a formidable opponent, weaving its tendrils through the fabric of our daily lives. It distorts reality, magnifies uncertainties, and casts shadows where there need be none. Yet, just as a passing storm cannot eternally shroud the sky, anxiety too is transient.

I want you to hold on to the unwavering truth that tomorrow is a promise, not a threat. As you navigate the anxious thoughts, remember that each step you take, no matter how small, brings you closer to the dawn of a new day. Your journey may be challenging but also a testament to your resilience.

Hidden beneath the surface of your struggles lies a wellspring of strength. In moments of doubt, when anxiety tightens its grip, recognise the courage it takes to face each day. Your strength, though unseen, is an undeniable force that will guide you through the darkest nights towards the brighter horizons awaiting you.

Anxiety often thrives on the illusion of permanence. It convinces us that our current state is an unchanging reality. But, my friend, emotions are ever-shifting, like the ocean's tides. The weight you carry today is not a life sentence but a fleeting moment in the grand tapestry of your life.

You don't need to face this journey alone. Reach out to the pillars of support around you, friends, family, communities or professionals who understand the nuances of anxiety. In their embrace, you'll find solace and the reassurance that your struggles do not define you.

As I leave you with these words, envision them as a beacon lighting your way through the storm. Believe in the promise of healing, the resilience of your spirit, and the transformative power of time. You are not alone on this journey, and the dawn you seek is patiently awaiting its moment to grace your sky.

Hold on, dear reader, for the story of your life is still unfolding, and within its pages, the triumph over anxiety is a tale yet to be told.

Much Love,

Lisa x

Journalling prompts to help explore and reflect:

Anxiety Recovery:

- Describe a recent situation that triggered anxiety. What were the specific thoughts and feelings you experienced?
- What are your coping mechanisms during anxious moments? What has been effective and helpful, and which would you like to improve?
- Three things that bring you a sense of calm or joy are... How can you incorporate them into my daily life to reduce anxiety?
- What are the patterns or triggers of your anxious thoughts? Are there any recurring themes or situations that consistently contribute to anxiety? What can you reframe them to?
- Write a letter to yourself during moments of anxiety, offering self- compassion and encouragement. What advice would you give to a friend going through a similar situation?

Self Belief

- List three things about yourself you're proud of.
- Explore any limiting beliefs you may hold about yourself. Where do these beliefs come from, and how do they impact your actions and decisions? How can you reframe them?
- Describe a time when you doubted yourself but still pushed through and succeeded. What did you learn from that experience?
- Write down five positive affirmations about yourself. Repeat them daily with intention and notice any shifts in your self-perception over time.

Self-Confidence:

- Reflect on a challenging situation where you felt confident. What was it that contributed to your confidence in that moment?
- Set a small, achievable goal for yourself. Outline the steps you'll take to accomplish it and celebrate your progress along the way.
- Identify areas where you tend to doubt yourself. What evidence exists to challenge these doubts, and how can you build confidence in those areas?
- Write a letter to your future, more confident self. Visualise the person you want to become and the steps you'll take to get there.
- Remember, the key to effective journaling is honesty and self-reflection.

You can find my active community page on Instagram @simply_anxious

My website www.simplyanxious.co.uk

My first book published in 2022 is 'Simply Anxious – Notes on Anxiety Recovery

Printed in Great Britain
by Amazon